Contents

Hello!	2
Meet the bugs	3
Sharing the Planet	4
How We Express Ourselves	16
How the World Works	28
How We Organize Ourselves	48
Where We Are In Place and Time	58
Who We Are	72
Glossary	88

Which type of bug is best with words?

A spelling bee!

I hope we're not bugging you!

Every PYP Agent needs a badge! Design your PYP Agents badge here.

PYP AGENTS

Hello!

Welcome to your *How, Where, Who, Share!* Workbook! Shade in the badge when you have mastered the transdisciplinary theme.

SHARING THE PLANET

HOW WE EXPRESS OURSELVES

HOW THE WORLD WORKS

HOW WE ORGANIZE OURSELVES

WHERE WE ARE IN PLACE AND TIME

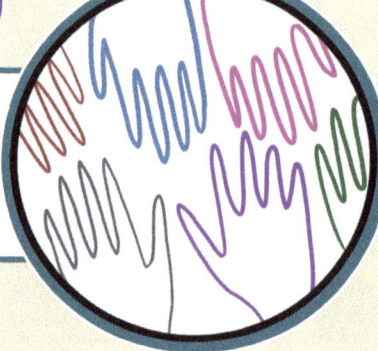

WHO WE ARE

Meet the bugs

You won't be on this journey alone. These bugs are PYP Agents too and they will guide you through this book with tips, jokes and interesting facts!

PRIM THE PRAYING MANTIS
Prim is not afraid to get things wrong. She is a **BALANCED RISK-TAKER**.

STIG THE STICK INSECT
Stig loves learning about our world and people! He is **KNOWLEDGEABLE** and **PRINCIPLED**.

BIA THE BEE
Bia likes to ask questions! She is an **INQUIRER** who is always **OPEN-MINDED**.

SEN THE SNAIL
Sen wonders why things are the way they are. She is **REFLECTIVE** and a **THINKER**.

GRANT THE GRASSHOPPER
Grant is very **CARING**. He is a **COMMUNICATOR** who loves to share his ideas.

CREATE YOUR OWN BUG HERE

Sharing the Planet

1 WATER, WATER EVERYWHERE... BUT HOW MUCH CAN WE DRINK?

Alaska, USA

Have you ever wondered what we would do if we didn't have water?

All living things need water to **survive**. Without it, there would be no plants, animals, seas, rivers – and no us!

The world's oceans store about 97% of our water, but have you ever accidentally drunk some sea water? Yuck! That is because sea water has salt in it. We can't drink salt water as it would make us ill, so where does our drinking water come from?

Did you know that frozen water is lighter than liquid water? That's why ice floats!

What would you like to know about water?
Write your questions here . . .

Germany

Wyoming, USA

Greenland

Why do sharks only swim in salt water?

Because pepper makes them sneeze!

5

THE WATER CYCLE

Can you remember the different states of matter that water can exist in?

1. ....

2. ....

3. ....

Water can be found in one of these states all over our planet. It is in the oceans, on land and in the **atmosphere**.

The water cycle shows us how water changes from one state into another.

Psst! For a clue, look at the pictures on page 5!

HINT

Why do you think the water cycle is important to life on Earth?

Water is the only substance on Earth found in three forms!

Taiwan

There are three stages of the water cycle:

- **Evaporation**
- **Condensation**
- **Precipitation**

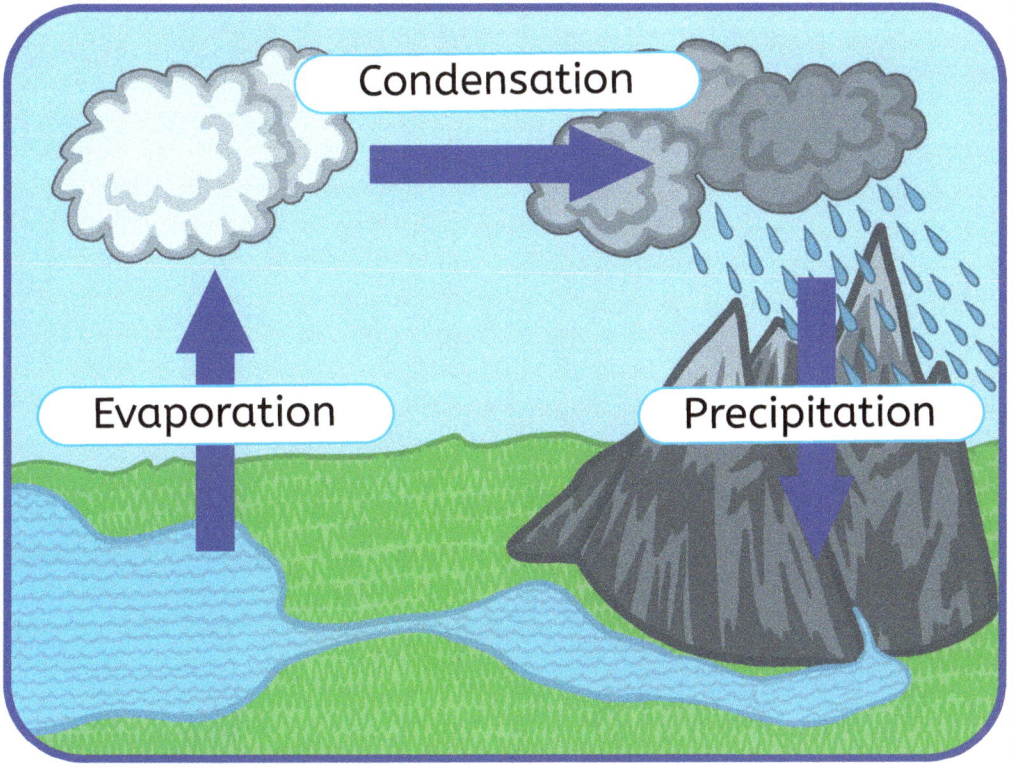

Water evaporates into the air by the heat of the Sun.

It cools down and condenses, forming clouds.

The clouds then fall back to the Earth as rain. This is called precipitation.

Finally, this water runs back into the ocean where the cycle starts all over again!

I wonder why clouds are different shapes . . .

On average, an adult uses 142 litres of water per day!

1. Create your own water cycle.

You could draw a diagram, create a model, or do something even more creative!

Remember to use and explain scientific words: condensation, evaporation and precipitation.

Why do you think the different states of matter are important to the water cycle?

SCIENCE EXPERIMENT

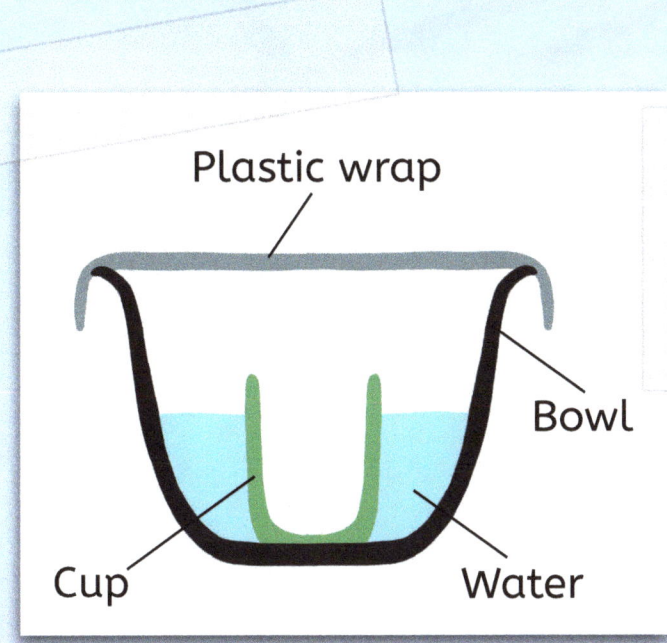

You will need:

- A clear plastic bowl
- A cup or a mug
- Plastic wrap
- Sticky tape
- Water
- A heat source (like sunlight or a lamp)

METHOD

1. Place your cup in the middle of your bowl.

2. Pour water into the bowl around your cup, making sure no water goes into your cup.

3. Cover the top with clear plastic wrap and secure with tape or a rubber band, making sure there are no gaps.

4. Put under a heat source like a heat lamp or outside if it is sunny.

5. Leave for the day, coming back now and again to observe what is happening.

PREDICTIONS

2. What do you think will happen to the water? Why?

....

....

....

....

....

....

3. What would happen if we put the bowl in the shade? Why?

....

....

....

....

....

....

It is much cooler in the shade!

Each day the sun evaporates a trillion tons of water. That's 400 million swimming pools!

OBSERVATIONS

4. Use the space below to record what you observe throughout the day.

> Remember to use scientific vocabulary such as condensation and evaporation.

5. Present your findings to your class. What did you observe?

THE LUXURY OF CLEAN, SAFE WATER

Water is so important to humans. If we don't get enough water, we become **dehydrated**. This can give us headaches and make us tired. Eventually, we can get extremely ill. We can last up to three weeks without food but only three days without water!

Water is also important to keep us clean. Our hands are a great place to pick up germs, so we need water to help clean them.

Unfortunately, in some countries people don't have access to clean water. This means they are drinking dirty water and cannot clean themselves properly. This is a life-threatening problem with many children dying because of it.

Many **communities** in these countries do not have a tap or well to give them water. They must get their water from their nearest river, which could be a long way from their home.

Millions of children miss school because of this as they need to help their family get water every day.

6. Why is it our responsibility to protect our water supply and keep it clean?

....
....
....
....
....
....
....
....

7. Is it everyone's responsibility to ensure everyone has access to clean water? Why do you think that?

....
....
....
....
....
....
....
....

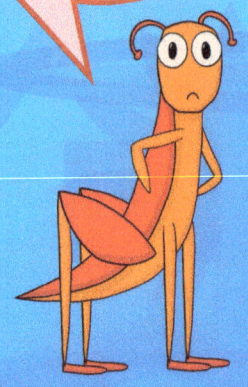

More than 1 billion people in the world do not have safe water to drink. That's every sixth person!

I wonder why it is such a challenge to protect our water supply and keep it clean?

RESEARCH SKILLS

8. Research how charities are helping to bring clean water to communities that need it.

Use this space to write down what you find.

....
....
....
....
....
....
....
....
....
....
....
....
....

9. Create a presentation of your choice about what you have found out.

Reflection

What have you learned?

New things I know

New things I can do

Now you can shade in your Sharing the Planet badge on page 2!

OVER TO YOU...

Have a look back at the questions you asked on page 5. Are there any questions that we haven't answered yet?

Now it is your turn to find the answers! Find out the answer to one of your questions and share what you have found with someone else.

How We Express Ourselves

2 SHARING STORIES

Have you ever wondered where stories come from? Sometimes they are completely made up, but other times they might be tales told to the storyteller when they were little. This is how stories are passed through the **generations** and how we know stories from many, many years ago.

We told stories to each other long before we wrote them into books. Have you ever seen images of cave paintings? That is the earliest form of storytelling. Some date back to 30,000 years ago!

What would you like to know about stories?
Write your questions here . . .

....

....

....

....

Lascaux, France

Humans painted images on caves to show animals, humans and other objects. This led to **oral** storytelling, passing down the tales from parents to their children, who then grew up and told their children. The stories contained knowledge and values that helped us to makes sense of the world and share that understanding with others.

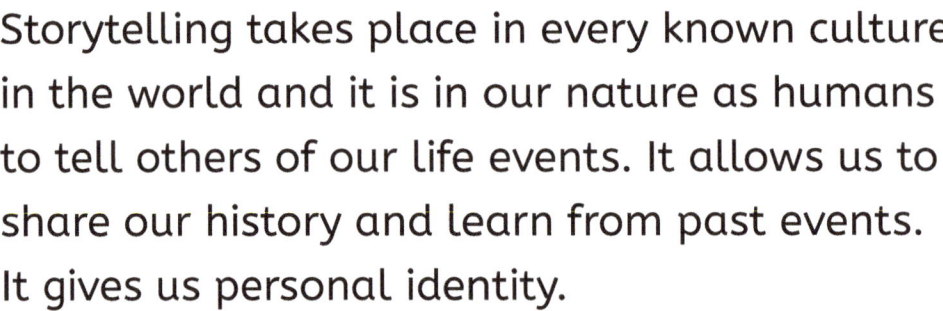

> You know the story of three little pigs who built their houses from straw, sticks and bricks? It was written in 1933!

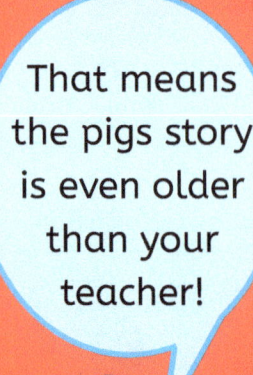

Storytelling takes place in every known culture in the world and it is in our nature as humans to tell others of our life events. It allows us to share our history and learn from past events. It gives us personal identity.

Even now, we tell stories every day. Imagine telling someone about your day at school – that's a story. Or if you turn on the TV and the news is telling us what is happening in the world. So is the reason you might give why you haven't done your homework!

Stories are as important to us now as they were in the past. But now we can use technology to tell and share them with people all over the world.

> That means the pigs story is even older than your teacher!

1. How do you think a story could be different depending on who is telling it?

....
....
....
....
....
....
....

2. Why do you think people read, write and tell stories?

....
....
....
....
....
....
....
....
....

The *Epic of Gilgamesh* is probably one of the first stories ever written down. It is thought to have been created in around 2100 BCE!

Stories can be made up or tell of real-life things that have happened.

Why do you think fables are told to children?

A famous collection of fables are called *Aesop's Fables*. It is thought they were created in Ancient Greece by a man called Aesop between 620 and 564 BCE!

FABLES

A fable is a type of story that was first told many years ago. They are short and usually involve animals who have human **characteristics**.

Have you ever heard of the stories 'The Boy Who Cried Wolf' or 'The Tortoise and the Hare'? These are both fables. At the end of the story, there is usually a **moral**. Sometimes this moral is made into a saying too. For example, in the fable 'The Tortoise and the Hare', the saying is 'slow and steady wins the race'.

Fables were often told as a way of offering people advice on how to live their lives. These stories show how actions can lead to consequences if chosen incorrectly.

The Tortoise and the Hare

The tortoise and the hare decided to have a race. The hare was much faster than the tortoise, and easily ran ahead. She was so sure she would win, she decided to have a nap. While the hare slept, the tortoise very slowly walked past and won the race.

The Boy Who Cried Wolf

A boy guarded his family's sheep. For fun, he shouted "WOLF! WOLF!" and all the villagers ran over to help. He laughed at them and they went away again, feeling very annoyed. When there was a real wolf, no one believed the boy when he called for help.

Features of a fable
- Fiction
- Short without many characters
- Characters are often animals who can talk
- Usually has a moral

3. The animals in fables often have the same characteristics. A lion would often be brave, a monkey would be mischievous and an owl would be wise.

What animal would you be? What characteristics would you have?

"You can find lots of fables online!"

"Why are fables still popular stories today?"

"I wonder why talking animals are used so much in fables."

RESEARCH SKILLS

4. Find some other examples of fables.

How did you find the fables?

....

....

....

....

5. Create a book cover for a fable. It can be one you already knew, your favourite one or a new one you have found.

Don't forget to write a blurb on the back!

6. Create your own comic strip retelling a different fable.

7. What is the moral of the story?

....
....
....
....

MYTHS

Myths are another type of story first told a long time ago. They were created by early civilizations to understand the world around them and explain how things were created. Back then, humans didn't understand a lot of the natural world like we do today. This meant they would create myths to explain things like thunder, a natural disaster or why their healthy crops suddenly died.

Features of a myth
- Fiction
- Short or long
- Characters often have supernatural powers
- Explains something in the world

In Greek mythology, the god of the sea is called Poseidon. He was known to have a bad temper. When he was angry, he would hit the floor with his trident, which would cause the ground to shake in an earthquake.

In Japan, myths blamed a gigantic catfish, or *namazu*, for earthquakes. This catfish was trapped underneath a stone that held him still. When his guard was distracted or asleep, the catfish shook his tail, causing earthquakes.

In Siberia, a god named Tuli drove a sledge that carried the Earth. This sledge was pulled by dogs that had fleas. When the dogs stopped to scratch at their fleas, it would shake the Earth and cause an earthquake.

8. Why do you think myths are still popular today?

....
....
....
....
....

9. How do you know?

....
....
....
....
....

10. Why do you think myths are different between countries and cultures?

....
....
....
....
....

In modern day, we use science to understand earthquakes.

Why were myths created?

You could use a story, myth or fable you know or write a new one.

The word 'atlas', which means a book of maps, comes from Greek myths. It is the name of a god called Atlas.

11. You are now going to do your own storytelling! Create and share your own story.

You need to choose how you are going to share your story. It could be written down, performed as a play, a poem, a dance or a song. Or something even more creative – it is up to you!

Write or plan your story here.

Reflection

What have you learned?

New things I know

New things I can do

Now you can shade in your How We Express Ourselves badge on page 2!

OVER TO YOU...

Have a look back at the questions you asked on page 16. Are there any questions that we haven't answered yet?

Now it is your turn to find the answers! Find out the answer to one of your questions and share what you have found with someone else.

How the World Works

3 OUR CHANGING PLANET

Have you ever been digging a hole and wondered what would happen if you kept digging down? Is it just soil and rocks beneath our feet? Is it lava – or is that only in volcanos? Actually, how are volcanos formed? And what about earthquakes? So many questions . . .

Luckily, you are in the right place to find the answers!

I think the whole earth is made of soil and rocks.

What would you like to know about the Earth? Write your questions here . . .

I think there is lava too!

The core is in the middle, like an apple core! Yum, apples!

And the crust is on the outside, like a piece of toast!

The mantle makes up 84% of the total volume of the Earth. That's a lot of molten rock!

THE EARTH

First, we need to know about the structure of the Earth! The Earth is made up of four different layers.

Inner core
Right at the centre of the Earth is a solid ball of metal. It is really hot here!

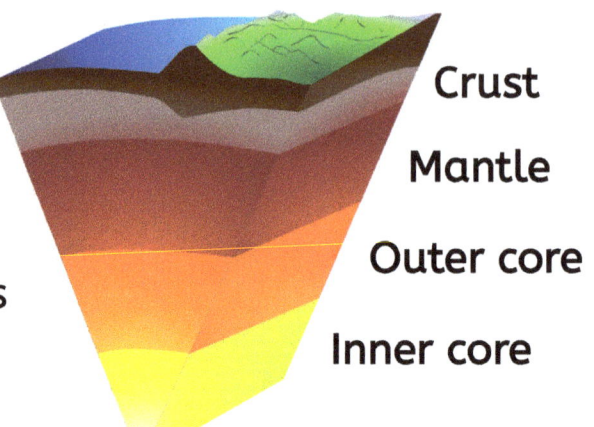

Crust
Mantle
Outer core
Inner core

Outer core
Around the inner core is liquid metal.

Mantle
Covering the core is lots of hot **molten** rock.

Crust
This covers the mantle. It is made up of lots of different pieces, a bit like a jigsaw puzzle!

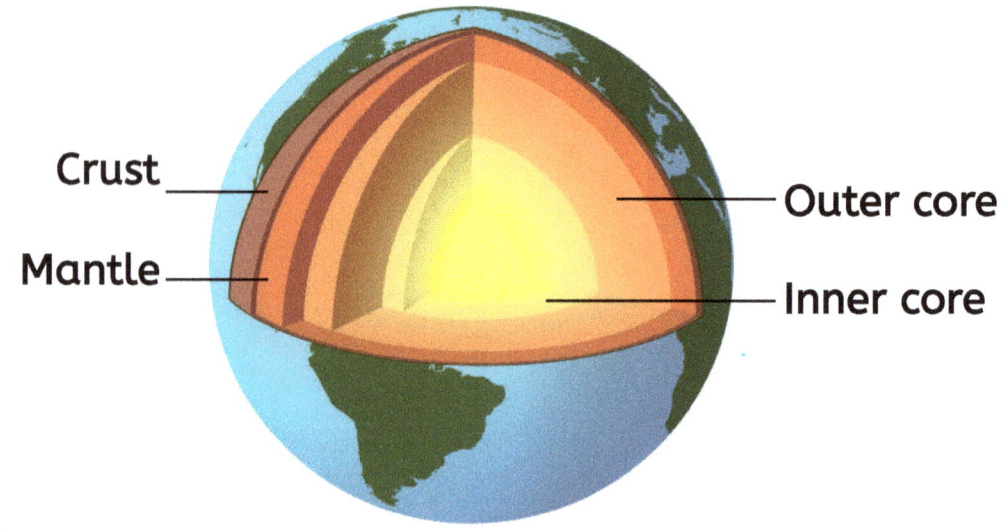

Crust
Mantle
Outer core
Inner core

1. Create your own 3D model of the Earth. Stick a picture of your model in the space below.

Add the scientific labels **inner core**, **outer core**, **mantle** and **crust** to your picture. Explain what they mean, too.

To understand earthquakes, we need to look closer at the crust of the Earth. Remember that the crust is made up of lots of pieces that fit together? The pieces are called **tectonic plates**.

Let's have a look at a tectonic plate map!

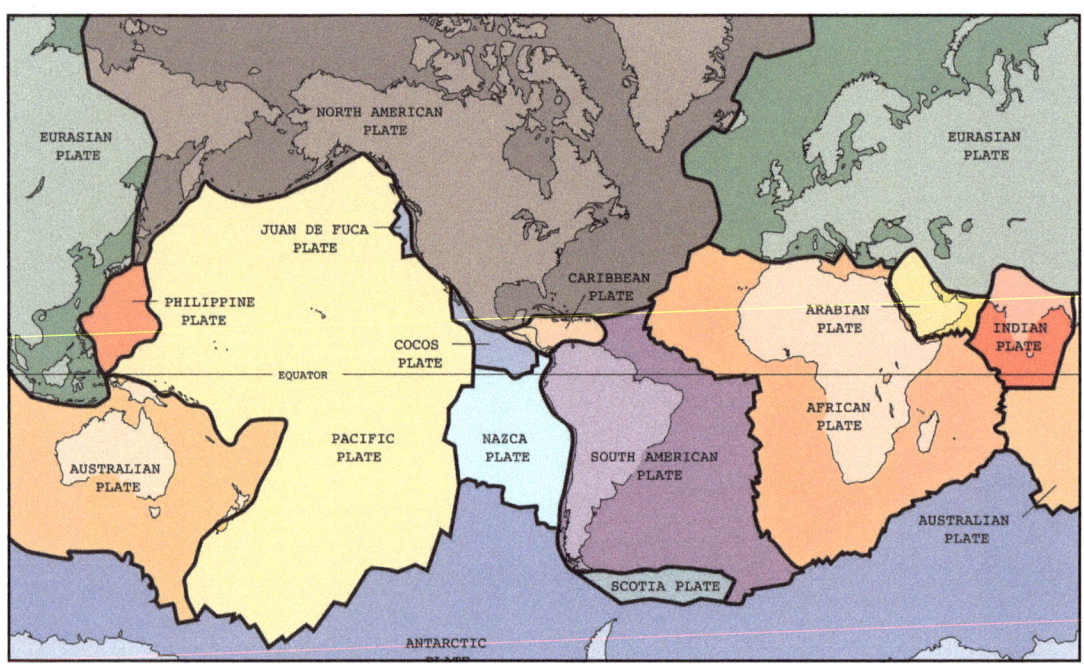

The plates are different sizes and they each have a name. Now look at this map. It shows where earthquakes are found.

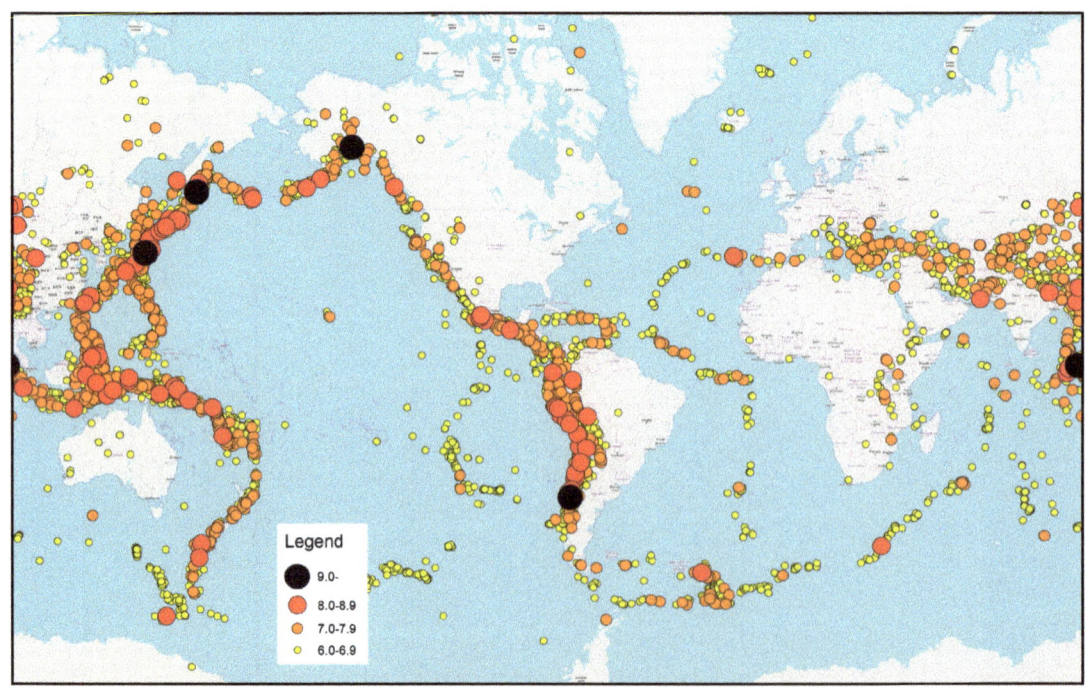

2. What do you notice about where earthquakes happen?

3. Why do you think this is?

Volcanoes often happen in the same places! I wonder why that is.

I think it is to do with the tectonic plates . . .

Earthquakes can cause huge ocean waves called tsunamis.

A tsunami can move at 500 miles per hour. That's as fast as a plane!

EARTHQUAKES

Now we know about tectonic plates. But how are they linked to earthquakes?

Tectonic plates are constantly moving. Sometimes they move towards each other, sometimes they move away from each other and sometimes they move alongside each other. The place where two tectonic plates meet is called a **fault**.

An earthquake can happen when a plate drags or bumps along another plate. Most of the time, the earthquake is too small for people to feel – but they can be powerful enough to be felt many miles away.

4. What causes an earthquake?

5. Why is it important that we understand how earthquakes are formed?

....

....

....

....

There are 7 major and 8 minor tectonic plates.

Each plate is on average 125 kilometres thick. That's taller than 30,000 African elephants stood on top of each other!

RESEARCH SKILLS

6. Research how people and communities have adapted to living in earthquake zones. Write down an amazing fact you have discovered!

My amazing fact!

....

....

....

....

Pick your side before you write.

Do cities have space for these buildings?

Do all countries have earthquakes?

7. In pairs, write a debate for or against the following question:

Should everyone have access to earthquake-proof buildings?

Are you **for** or **against** the question?

....

Write your debate here.

....
....
....
....
....
....
....
....
....
....
....
....
....
....

Alaska, USA

Nepal

I think everyone deserves to be safe.

Is this more important than other isues in a country?

SEISMOGRAPH

We measure an earthquake's **intensity** and **duration** using a **seismograph**.

CREATING A SEISMOGRAPH

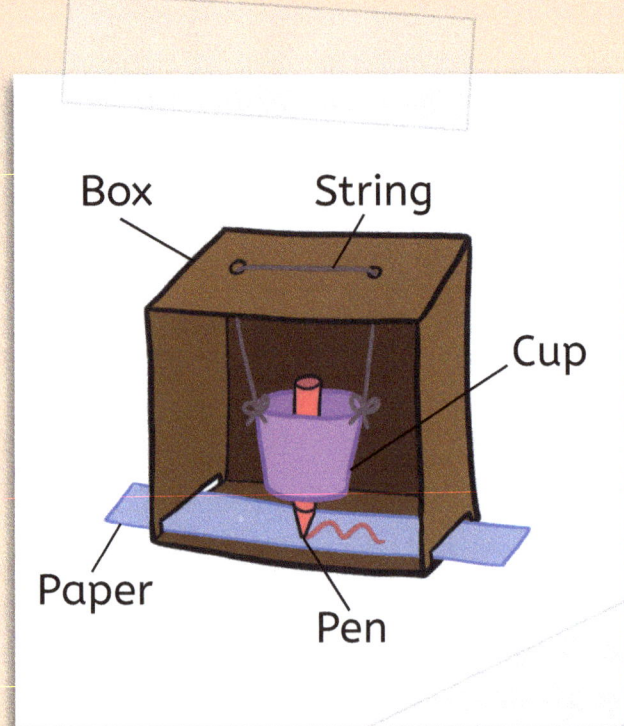

You will need:

- A shoebox (or similar)
- Paper or plastic cup
- 2 pieces of 40 cm string
- Marker pen
- Scissors
- Modelling clay or small stones
- Sticky tape
- Long strips of paper

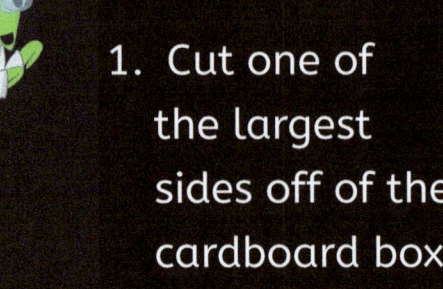

Ask an adult to help with the cutting!

METHOD

1. Cut one of the largest sides off of the cardboard box.

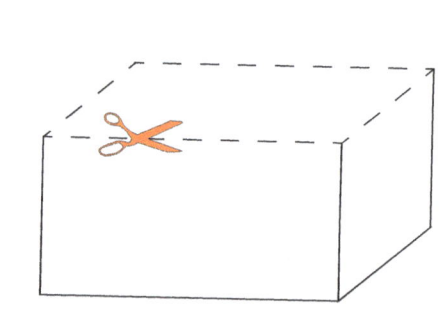

2. Make a hole in the bottom of your cup and a hole either side of the rim.

3. Tie a piece of string through each of the holes. The string needs to be slightly longer than the box.

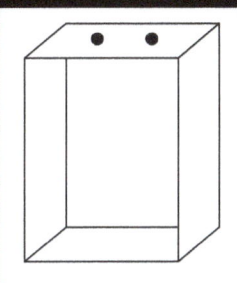

4. Make two holes in the top of the box. They need to be the same distance apart as the holes in the cup.

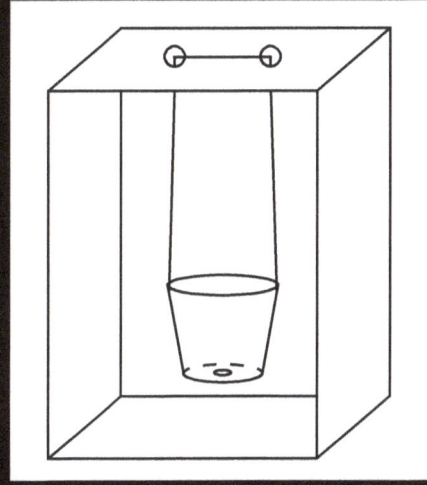

5. Push the two pieces of string through the holes and tie them together on the top of the box. This makes the cup hang down inside the box. The bottom of the cup should be slightly above the bottom of the box.

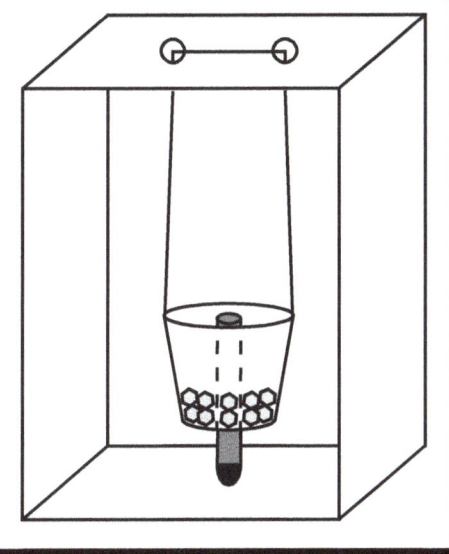

6. Push the marker through the hole at the bottom of the cup so its tip just touches the bottom of the box.

7. Place some modelling clay or small stones inside of the cup. They will act as a weight. Make sure the marker stays upright.

8. Cut long strips of paper and tape them together on one side to form one long strip of paper.

9. Cut two slits on opposite sides of the cardboard box as close to the bottom as possible. Your strip of paper goes through the slits.

10. Use the cup strings to make sure the marker is only just touching the paper.

11. Start using your seismograph!

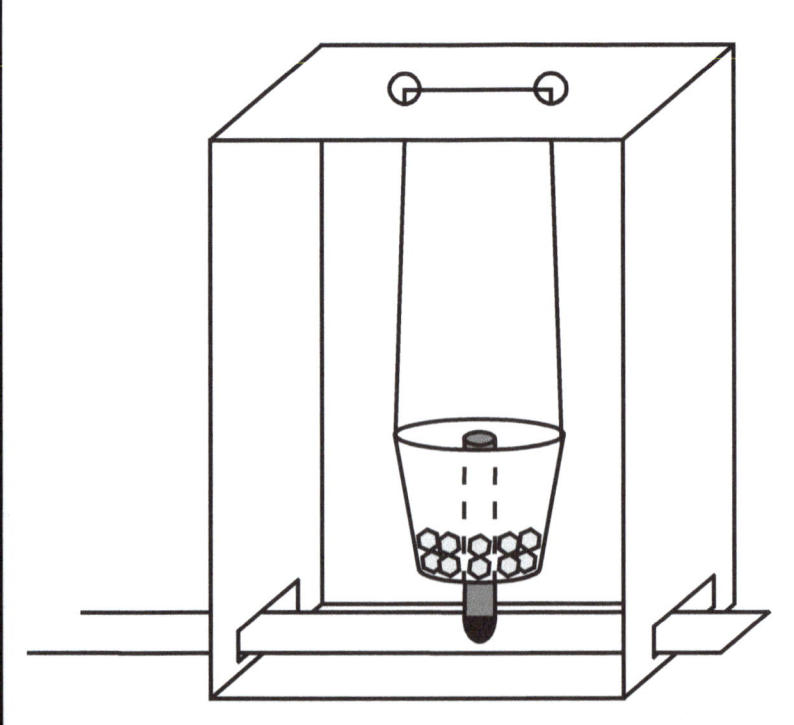

USING THE SEISMOGRAPH

The first person should hold the box. The second person should slowly pull the paper strip through the slits. The pen should leave a line on the paper.

Now, the first person should gently shake the box. The second person should keep pulling the paper at the same speed.

8. What do you notice happen to the lines made on the paper?

....
....
....

9. What happens if you shake the box more?

....
....
....
....

10. Carry your seismograph around with you for a few days and record different activities.

You should work in pairs!

Activities might be walking, running or travelling in a car.

11. How do we read a seismograph?

12. Which of your activities caused the widest lines?

13. Which activity caused the least amount of movement?

14. Why is it important to measure the strength of earthquakes?

VOLCANOES

A volcano erupting is very exciting and dangerous. But why aren't they erupting all the time? And why do some people live so close to them?

To understand volcanoes, we have to look at the structure of the Earth again. Do you remember that the mantle is made up of hot molten rock? This rock is called **magma**. The magma is looking for ways to escape up to the Earth's surface and when it does a volcano is formed.

There are three main ways that magma escapes to the Earth's surface. Two ways involve those tectonic plates again!

1 If the tectonic plates **collide** head on with each other (instead of sliding past each other), then a volcano can form as one plate is pushed under the other plate.

2 If the tectonic plates move away from each other, the magma can come up to the surface through the gap that is made.

3 If there is a weakness in the Earth's crust, then magma can push its way through. This is how you get volcanoes in the middle of tectonic plates.

Hawaii, USA

There are 1,500 volcanoes on Earth that are classed as active. This means they might erupt at any time!

A volcano eruption is when the magma escapes (or erupts) to the Earth's surface. This magma is now called **lava**. As the lava flows, it cools down and hardens to form rocks. Over time, this builds up and makes the volcano even bigger!

Volcanoes can cause a lot of damage to people and habitats, but there are some positives too. The ash that is made when an eruption happens is good fertilizer for soil, which makes it easier to grow plants and food. Volcanoes also bring many tourists to the area. The tourists spend their money in local businesses, which helps the local economy.

15. Why do you think volcanic ash clouds are a problem in so many countries?

....
....
....
....
....
....

I think our work on the water cycle will help answer this one!

HINT

16. Why do you think people live near volcanos?

Does everyone have a choice about where they live?

....
....
....
....
....
....
....
....

17. You are visiting a volcano whilst on holiday. Write a postcard home to a person of your choice, explaining what you can see and how the volcano has been formed.

POSTCARD

RESEARCH SKILLS

18. Research which agencies help deal with natural disasters.

Think about the following questions to help get you started:

- What do the agencies do when a natural disaster happens?

- Who helps pay for the agencies or their equipment and supplies? Are they charities or funded another way?

- Who do you think should pay for them? Should it be the countries they are helping or should it be a worldwide responsibility?

Make your notes here, but it is your choice how you present your findings. You could make a poster, a presentation or something even more creative!

What would you have in your own survival kit?

Reflection

What have you learned?

New things I know

New things I can do

Now you can shade in your How the World Works badge on page 2!

OVER TO YOU...

Have a look back at the questions you asked on page 28. Are there any questions that we haven't answered yet?

Now it is your turn to find the answers! Find out the answer to one of your questions and share what you have found with someone else.

How We Organize Ourselves

4 COMPARING COMMUNITIES

Did you know that communities are all around us? In every **culture** and in every country, there are lots of communities. A community is a group of people with something in common. This could be a similar interest, where you live, a job you do, or something else. There are so many different types of communities!

Why do we have communities?

What would you like to know about communities? Write your questions here . . .

....

....

....

....

What are some synonyms for community? A thesaurus could help!

HINT

There are many reasons why we form communities. It could be to sell things, to work together, to make people feel safe or for religious beliefs. To be a valuable part of a community, we must learn how to respect and work with others. By doing this, we can solve problems that are too big for one person.

1. Everyone belongs to some communities. Which ones do you belong to?

....

....

....

Do you belong to any sports clubs, online clubs or group activities?

2. Look at the outline of the hand below.

- Inside the hand, write words or draw pictures that represent you.

- Outside the hand, write words or draw pictures that represent the communities you belong to.

3. Compare your picture with your friends' pictures. Think about what is the same and what is different.

Add any communities you missed to your picture.

4. What buildings/structures/people would be in your ideal community? Make your notes here!

....
....
....
....
....

5. Make your own model of your ideal community. You could use clay, cardboard or something else!

Stick a picture of your model here.

I wonder how communities online are the same and different to ones we have in person.

I'm going to build my community out of building blocks!

What values do you think a community should have?

Why is your model different or the same?

6. What makes your community special?

7. Compare your community model to your partner's model. How are they similar? How are they different?

HOW DO COMMUNITIES CHANGE OVER TIME?

The communities we have today aren't always the same as we would have had if we lived fifty or a hundred years ago. For example, the internet only started to be used in homes in the 1990s!

Every community has a history, but they also grow and change over time. This can be due to things like new technology, people or natural resources. For example, when people started using cars instead of horses to move around, this changed communities. Roads had to be made bigger and were eventually paved. People could travel to different places quicker in cars, so they were able to meet others and trade goods further away. It also meant that people could move out of towns, creating more villages.

Can you think of a major event that could change a community?

Is it important for communities to change over time?

Is your life similar or different to their way of life?

Are any communities around now that weren't around then? Why do you think this is?

RESEARCH SKILLS

8. Interview an older adult about their way of life when they grew up.

- How did their family and community live and work together?

- Did they belong to any online communities?

- Did they have to go to school?

9. Create a Venn diagram showing the similarities and differences between their communities and your communities.

COMMUNITIES AND COUNTRIES

Think about the last place you travelled to. Where was it? Was it similar to where you live or was it different? The place we live in, and the culture we are a part of, can mean we belong to different types of communities. A child living in the centre of the city of Tokyo may belong to different communities to a child living in a small village in Ethiopia.

Think about where you live. There can be many communities that make up where you live. Your family, your school, the city/town where you live and the country you live in are all communities which belong to you.

What communities do they have?

How are their lives similar and different to yours?

10. Your task is to compare your communities with those from a child in another country.

You will first need to research a different country. Which country have you chosen?

Make your research notes here.

....
....
....
....
....
....
....
....
....
....

11. Now compare their communities to your own. It is up to you how you present your findings.

You could do an essay, a table, a presentation, a poster, or something even more creative!

Reflection

What have you learned?

New things I know

New things I can do

Now you can shade in your How We Organize Ourselves badge on page 2!

OVER TO YOU...

Have a look back at the questions you asked on page 48. Are there any questions that we haven't answered yet?

Now it is your turn to find the answers! Find out the answer to one of your questions and share what you have found with someone else.

Where We Are in Place and Time

5 WHY EGYPTIANS LOVED THEIR MUMMIES

Look at these pictures. Can you tell what **civilization** they come from? There wasn't any modern machinery all those years ago, so how did they manage to build such big pyramids? Where did they get the rock from if they are built on sand? And how do we know so much about them if they lived so long ago?

You might have guessed that these images are from the Ancient Egyptians. The pyramids are famous around the world and are one of the seven wonders of the ancient world.

What would you like to know about Ancient Egypt? Write your questions here . . .

....

....

....

....

TIMELINE

I can't remember what BCE and CE stands for!

7000 BCE	3000 BCE	2700 BCE	2630 BCE	2200 BCE
A group of famers live next to the River Nile in Egypt.	Narmer joined Egypt and created the capital, Memphis.			

MAKING A KINGDOM

Long before the Ancient Egyptians (around 7000 BCE), there was already a group of farmers living next to the River Nile. Egypt was split into two, called Lower Egypt and Upper Egypt. Then in 3000 BCE the first Egyptian **pharaoh** called Narmer (also known as Menes) joined both parts of Egypt together and made a capital called Memphis where the two lands met. This was the first capital of Egypt.

| 2100 BCE | 1800 BCE | 1500 BCE | 1000 BCE | 30 BCE |

While the Ancient Egyptians lived, there were three main time periods that were known as kingdoms. They were called the Old Kingdom, Middle Kingdom and New Kingdom.

Old Kingdom

The Old Kingdom lasted from about 2700 BCE until 2200 BCE. During this time, the Egyptians created hieroglyphics and built the pyramids.

As we learn more about Ancient Egypt, you will be able to add more events to your timeline!

Why is Tutankhamun so well known?

Middle Kingdom

The Middle Kingdom lasted from 2100 BCE until 1800 BCE.

During this time, pharaohs were starting to be buried in hidden tombs instead of pyramids.

New Kingdom

The New Kingdom was from 1500 BCE until 1000 BCE. This is known as the Egyptian golden age. There were lots of wealth and building projects during this time, and the capital was moved to Thebes. This was when the famous pharaoh Tutankhamun lived. Pharaohs were buried in tombs in the area known as the Valley of the Kings.

The Ancient Egyptian period ended in 30 BCE, when a famous ruler named Cleopatra died.

1. Look at the timeline on the last page.

Plot the beginning and end of the three kingdoms on the timeline.

PHARAOHS

Pharaohs were the rulers of Ancient Egypt. Generally, men were more likely to become pharaohs, but the pharaoh's wife was also an important ruler and was usually called the 'Great Royal Wife'. Sometimes the wife became more well-known than the pharaoh! When a woman became the ruler, she would still keep the title of pharaoh.

The title of pharaoh would usually pass to the oldest son of the current pharaoh. He would go through training to make sure he would be a good leader when the time came.

2. What do you think would make someone a good pharaoh?

....
....
....
....

Hatshepsut was a powerful female pharaoh. She wore a fake beard to appear more kingly.

Cleopatra is the most well-known female pharaoh. According to legend, she bathed in donkey milk to keep her skin soft.

RESEARCH SKILLS

Pharaohs would often link themselves to a god or goddess to appear more powerful.

Cleopatra chose Isis, goddess of healing and magic.

I wonder what other Ancient Egyptian gods there are.

3. Research the different pharaohs of Ancient Egypt and create your own set of fact cards about them. You can use the template below to help you or make up your own.

Name
_____

Dates ruled
_____

Interesting facts
_____
_____
_____
_____

4. Add when your pharaohs ruled on to your timeline.

SCIENCE EXPERIMENT

Here are the steps to make a mummy. Follow them to mummify a tomato!

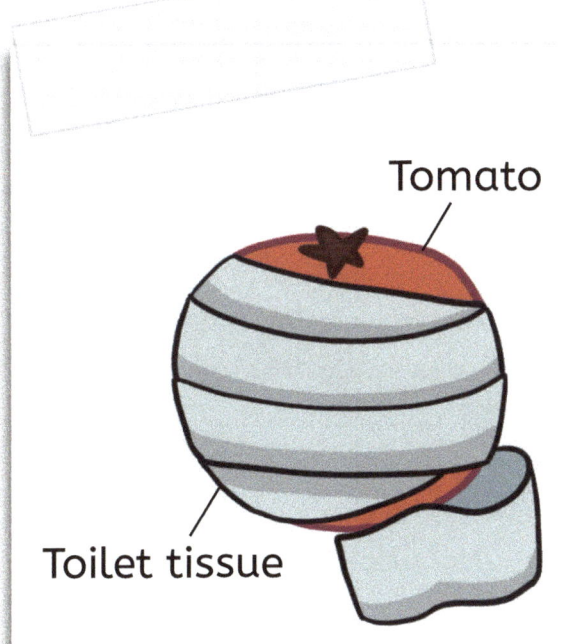

You will need:

- A large tomato
- A small teaspoon
- Salt
- Antibacterial hand gel
- A clear plastic bag
- A knife (and an adult!)
- A paper clip
- Toilet tissue or similar

METHOD

1. **Ancient Egyptians hooked the brain out through the nose** Bend the paper clip into a hook and make a small hole where the stalk of the tomato was. After breaking apart the 'brains', try and hook some bits out.

2. **The organs were then pulled out through a little cut**
Now you are ready to cut open the body and remove the organs. Make a small cut into your tomato and scoop out the guts using a small teaspoon.

3. **The body needed to be washed carefully with alcohol to make sure it did not rot**
Use antibacterial gel and give your tomato a good clean, inside and out.

4. **The body was filled with a special salt to ensure it was dried out and ready to be wrapped**

Put your prepared tomato into your clear, plastic bag and add salt. Make sure the inside of the tomato is filled up with salt.

5. **The body was covered and left for forty days**
Seal the bag and leave for forty days in the sunlight.

6. **The body was wrapped in long strips of cloth**
Wrap your tomato mummy in toilet tissue. Now it is ready to go in its sarcophagus and tomb.

5. Take a photograph or draw a picture of your tomato before it is mummified, after forty days, and after it is wrapped.

Before	40 days	Wrapped

6. Describe your tomato at each stage. Include how it feels and smells. Write this on the lines below your pictures.

7. Would this work with other vegetables/fruit? Why do you think that?

What would happen if you don't add the salt?

HIEROGLYPHICS

From very early on, the Ancient Egyptians used their own form of written language. These are called hieroglyphics and are made up of pictures. To be able to write in hieroglyphics, you had to go to a special school and learn to become a *scribe*.

It was a tricky job. Hieroglyphics could be written right to left, left to right, vertically or horizontally!

8. Use this space to make your own hieroglyphic alphabet.

A	B	C	D	E

F	G	H	I	J

K	L	M	N	O	P

Q	R	S	T	U

V	W	X	Y	Z

9. Write a message using your hieroglyphic alphabet.

Give your message to a partner to work out!

10. There is a major difference between our alphabet and the Ancient Egyptian alphabet. What do you think it is?

Keep the images simple! You might need to draw them lots of times to write a sentence.

HINT

There are over 700 different hieroglyphics! Some pictures mean different words and other pictures mean **phonetic** sounds.

ANCIENT EGYPTIAN TECHNOLOGY

Have you ever been brushing your teeth and wondered who first used toothpaste? Was it always mint flavour? Without toothpaste in our lives, our mouths wouldn't be clean or minty fresh – and we must thank the Ancient Egyptians for this. It is thought that they started using toothpaste around 500 BCE. But they didn't just invent toothpaste. Ancient Egyptians were great inventors, with a lot of their inventions still used today.

RESEARCH SKILLS

11. Research one piece of Ancient Egyptian technology that we still use today.

Think about why it was invented and how it is used in modern times. How would the modern world be different without this invention? It is up to you how you present your research.

Reflection

What have you learned?

New things I know

New things I can do

OVER TO YOU...

Now you can shade in your Where We Are in Place and Time badge on page 2!

Have a look back at the questions you asked on page 58. Are there any questions that we haven't answered yet?

Now it is your turn to find the answers! Find out the answer to one of your questions and share what you have found with someone else.

Who We Are

6 ME AND MY EMOTIONS

Have you ever seen a toddler having a tantrum in the street? Your friend crying when they have hurt themselves? Or someone laughing so much they have tears rolling down their face? As humans, we have a wide range of **emotions** that start being expressed as soon as we are born.

As we get older, we experience more and more emotions that can **influence** our lives. From the decisions we make to how we interact with other people, our emotions play an important role in our lives.

But sometimes we don't know how to control them. Learning about the different types of emotions and their influence on you, will help you to understand how these feelings affect your behaviour.

What do you call an angry pea?

Grumpy!

What would you like to know about emotions?
Write your questions here . . .

....

....

....

....

1. Look at the pictures below. Underneath each picture, write one word that explains how the picture makes you feel.

2. Everyone can feel differently about things.

Look at the picture of the rollercoaster again. For some people, the emotion would be excitement or happiness. Other people would look at it and feel fear.

Look at the word you wrote. Why did the picture make you feel that way?

....

....

3. Humans have a lot of emotions! How many emotions can you think of? Write them on the mind map below.

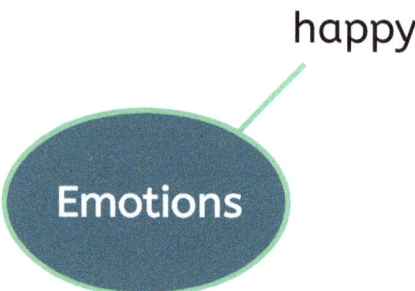

REPRESENTING

Remember the images we looked at and how they can give people different emotions? Colours, objects and sounds can do this too.

Some people feel happy when they look at the ocean and listen to the waves. Blue is also seen as a calming colour.

4. Think of all the sounds that you can. Decide if they make you feel a positive emotion or a negative emotion, and add them to the table.

Which objects and sounds make you feel happy?

Positive sounds	Negative sounds
Ocean waves	Car alarm

What you feel may be different to what someone else feels!

5. Look at the coloured boxes below. Inside each box, write one emotion that you think of when you see that colour.

HOW ELSE CAN WE REPRESENT EMOTIONS?

Line drawings can represent emotions. Look at the line below.

6. Does this feel calm or angry to you? Why?

....
....
....

7. What emotion does the line below make you think of? Why?

....
....
....
....

8. Draw what you think a calm line might look like.

9. Design a room with objects in it that would make you feel calm and relaxed. You could draw it below, create it on a computer or make a model.

10. Choose one of the objects from your room and explain why you chose it. How does it make you feel?

Remember to think about the colours you would choose.

I'm going to put a beanbag chair and fairy lights in my room!

I like the colour blue. It makes me feel calm and reminds me of the sounds of the ocean.

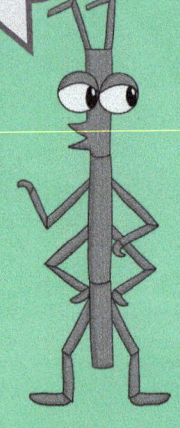

My angry mood monster is going to be little, spiky and red.

My happy mood monster is going to be rounded and smiley.

11. Create a mood monster that shows an emotion you have felt at some time. It is up to you which emotion it shows and what you make it from. Think about its shape and colours.

Draw a picture or stick in a picture of your mood monster.

12. Why did you choose this emotion for your monster?

....
....
....

13. How did you make your monster look like your emotion?

....
....

14. Share your monster with a partner. How are they the same? How are they different?

....
....
....
....

15. Compare your monster with someone else who chose the same emotion. Do your monsters look similar or different? Why?

....
....
....
....

HELPING TO CONTROL OUR EMOTIONS

Emotions and feelings are an everyday part of life, but sometimes these emotions can feel very strong. It is important for us to know what these feelings are and understand how they influence us in positive and negative ways.

16. Talk to a partner about a time you had an emotion that affected you in a negative way. Then discuss a time when you had an emotion that affected you in a positive way. Be prepared to share with the class!

Managing emotions is hard, whether you are seven or seventy! This means it is important to know when you are feeling certain emotions and what you can do to help control those feelings.

Have you ever seen a footballer or soccer player before they take a penalty? You might see them taking deep breaths. This is because they are very nervous, but they have learnt that taking deep breaths can help calm them down.

I do some colouring if I am feeling sad.

I listen to music if I am feeling angry.

I talk to an adult if I am feeling upset.

Have you ever felt your heart beating fast when you are nervous or angry? Taking deep breaths can help with this too. It makes you focus on taking breaths and not on your feelings. It also slows down your **heartbeat**, which can also calm you down.

Exercise can also help manage our emotions. Some people like to go for a run. Other people prefer slower, calmer activities like yoga. Is there an exercise you like to do if you are feeling a strong emotion?

17. Why is it important that we have strategies to control our emotions?

....

....

....

....

18. Are there any situations when being angry can be a positive thing?

....

....

....

....

19. Discuss with a partner what you do to remain calm and relaxed. Write any ideas here.

....

....

....

....

Norway

RESEARCH SKILLS

20. Research different ways you can control your emotions and make your notes below.

Pick how you want to present what you have learnt. You could design a poster, make an instruction sheet, film a video, sing a song or anything else!

EXPRESSING OUR EMOTIONS THROUGH ART

Art of any kind can show the emotions of an artist and make us feel a certain way. The colours used, as well as what and how the artist is painting, can mean the art feels moody or happy, excited or calm.

Jackson Pollock was an American artist who is known for making *Abstract Expressionism* art. Abstract means that the artist isn't trying to paint a picture to make objects look real and Expressionism is a type of art that expresses thoughts and emotions.

Pollock was famous for covering large canvases in different colours of paint. His paintbrushes never touched his canvas – instead, he dripped the paint from the paintbrush straight on to canvases that were placed on the floor. He did not plan his work. Instead, he painted following his thoughts and emotions.

21. Research the work of Jackson Pollock. Try to find some videos of him painting to see how he produced his art.

Do you like his artwork? Why or why not?

22. What is your favourite piece of art by him? Why?

....

....

....

23. How do you think he expresses his emotions in his art?

....

....

....

24. Now it's your turn! Create your own piece of Abstract Expressionism artwork. Don't forget to sign it.

Take a picture of your finished piece and stick it in the picture frame.

25. What do you think about the painting you created? What do you like or dislike?

26. What thoughts or emotions were you trying to show in your painting? How did you do this?

Artwork by Steve Johnson

27. Look at the mind map you completed on page 74. Are there any other emotions you would like to add to it? Write these in a different colour.

28. Discuss with a partner to fill in the flow chart of things you could do to calm down if you are getting angry or frustrated.

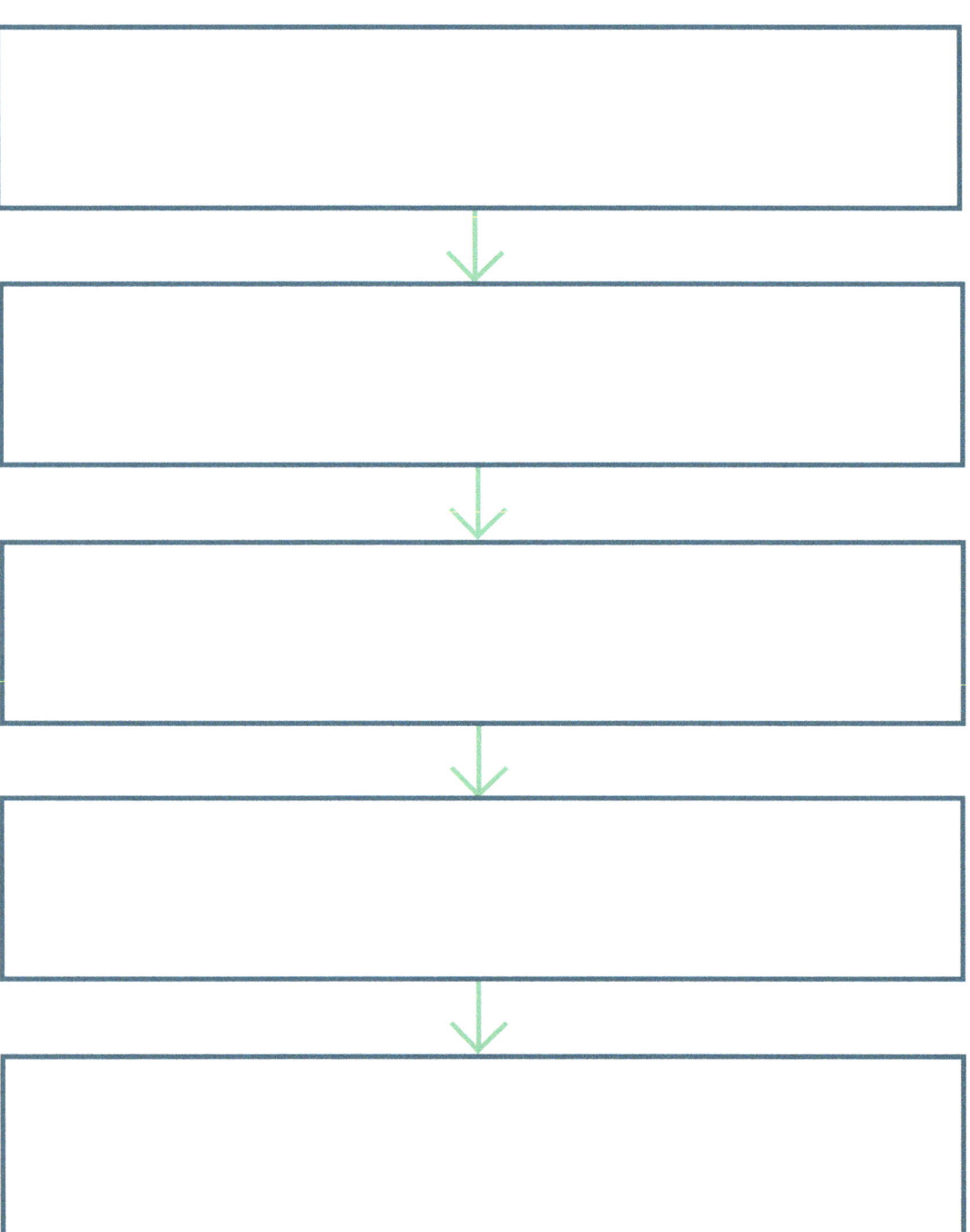

Reflection

What have you learned?

- New things I know
- New things I can do

Now you can shade in your Who We Are badge on page 2!

OVER TO YOU . . .

Have a look back at the questions you asked on page 73. Are there any questions that we haven't answered yet?

Now it is your turn to find the answers! Find out the answer to one of your questions and share what you have found with someone else.

Glossary

Atmosphere the gases surrounding a planet

Characteristics features belonging to a person, place or thing

Civilization a group of people that have their own language and way of life

Collide violently hit something

Communities a group of people living in the same place

Condensation/Condenses change from a gas to a liquid

Culture the way of life for a group of people

Dehydrated when your body does not have enough water

Duration how long something lasts

Emotion a strong feeling

Evaporation/Evaporates when liquid water becomes vapour

Fault a place where tectonic plates meet

Generations people born and living around the same time

Heartbeat the pulse of a heart

Influence the effect it has on something

Intensity how strong something is

Lava magma on the Earth's surface

Magma molten rock beneath the surface of the Earth

Molten heated up so much it has turned to liquid

Moral a lesson that can be learnt from a story

Oral spoken

Pharaoh a ruler of Ancient Egypt

Phonetic uses sounds

Precipitation/Precipitate water that falls to the ground as rain

Seismograph instrument which measures how strong an earthquake is

Survive continue to live

Published by Extend Education Ltd.,
Alma House, 73 Rodney Road, Cheltenham, UK GL50 1HT
www.extendeducation.com

The right of Harriet Wittmann to be identified as author of this work has been asserted by them with the Copyright, Designs and Patents Act 1988.

Cover art based on a photograph by Chaz McGregor

First published 2021
25 24 23 22 21
10 9 8 7 6 5 4 3 2 1
ISBN 978-1-913121-37-2

Printed in the UK

Copyright notice

All rights reserved. No part of this publication may be reproduced, stored in a retrieval system or transmitted in any form or by any means, electronic, mechanical, photocopying, recording or otherwise, without permission in writing from the copyright owner, except in accordance with the provisions of the Copyright, Designs and Patents Act 1988 or under the terms of a licence from the Copyright Licensing Agency Limited. Further details of such licences (for reprographic reproduction) may be obtained from the Copyright Licensing Agency Limited, Barnard's Inn, 86 Fetter Lane, London EC4A 1EN (www.cla.co.uk). Applications for the copyright owner's written permission should be addressed to the publisher.

Permissions

4: McKayla Crump; **5:** Tanja Cotoaga, Annie Spratt, Emily Campbell, Lee Jeffs; **6:** Giorgio Trovato, Vicky Ng; **10:** Kenrick Mills; **12:** Kayla Gibson, CDC, Frank Albrecht; **17:** Prof saxx (CC BY-SA 3.0); **29:** USGS; **30:** Washiucho (CC BY-SA 4.0), Mats Halldin (CC BY-SA 3.0); **32:** Phoenix7777 (CC BY-SA 4.0); **37:** NOAA, Punya (CC BY-SA 4.0); **42 & 43:** Steve Halama; **49:** Church of the King, Austin Nicomedez, Annie Spratt, Museums Victoria, Amish Thakkar, Randy Fath, Robert Bye, Calin Stan; **52 & 53:** Boston Public Library; **59:** Jeremy Bezanger, AussieActive, British Library, Leonardo Ramos; **61:** Alex Azabache; **62:** AussieActive, Robert Thiemann; **63:** Jeff Dahl (CC BY-SA 4.0); **66:** engin akyurt; **68 & 69:** Tom Podmore; **72:** Tengyart; **73:** Count Chris, Ray Hennessy, Eric Ward, Casey Horner, Matt Bowden, Max LaRochelle; **75:** Sean Oulashin; **80 & 81:** Julia Caesar; **84:** Wellcome Images (CC BY 4.0); **84 & 85:** Steve Johnson.

www.ingramcontent.com/pod-product-compliance
Lightning Source LLC
Chambersburg PA
CBHW041633040426
42446CB00025B/3499